Kinsey Scale for the Emotionally Fragile Queer

Bibi June

Burning Eye

Burning Eye Books
Never Knowingly
Mainstream

Copyright © 2022 Bibi June

The author asserts the moral right under the Copyright, Designs and Patents Act 1988 to be identified as the author of this work.

All rights reserved. No part of this publication may be reproduced, stored in a retrieval system, or transmitted, in any form or by any means without the prior written consent of the author, nor be otherwise circulated in any form of binding or cover other than that in which it is published and without a similar condition being imposed on the subsequent purchaser.

This first edition published by Burning Eye Books 2022

www.burningeye.co.uk

@burningeyebooks

Burning Eye Books
15 West Hill, Portishead, BS20 6LG

ISBN 978-1-913958-24-4

Bibi June is a poet and performance maker whose work focuses on queerness, climate justice and post-apocalyptic stories. They work as a producer on spoken word and immersive performances, and their creative work spans from poetry to games to theatre. Their writing work has been published in places such as Gutter, We Were Always Here and Ceremony. 'Kinsey Scale' is their fourth pamphlet. Their first pamphlet about queer joy, 'Begin Again', was published by Speculative Books in 2018. In 2020, their second pamphlet 'Critique of the Criminal Justice System' was published by Stewed Rhubarb. It was nominated for the Callum Macdonald Memorial Award in 2021. Their third pamphlet came out in 2021, titled 'TransMask: A DIY Zine for Queers of the Apocalypse'.

Together with Ross McFarlane and Ellen Renton, they run spoken word theatre company In The Works. Their previous collaborative shows include 'A Matter of Time' (2017) and 'The 900 Club', the latter of which received 4* and 5* reviews for its debut run at the Edinburgh Fringe. In 2019, they toured their newest collaborative show 'Make/Shift' with Ross at theatres and spoken word events across the UK & Ireland. It was adapted into an audio drama for the Saboteur Awards Festival in early 2020. They work on award-winning queer horror podcast Folxlore.

The Kinsey Scale is an archaic measure of queerness, created in 1948 as a way of putting a number on someone's sexuality. It ranges from zero, perfectly straight, to six, devastatingly homosexual, and includes a category X, for people who do not experience any sexual attraction (something we now call asexuality).

This scale is not and was never fit for purpose. It does not encompass the wholeness of queer experiences, the nuance of them, the joys and terrors, the genderfuckery and sexy hot mess that queerness can be.

We deserve more.

This is a rewrite of the original Kinsey Scale.
An attempt, an undoing.

This is *Kinsey Scale for the Emotionally Fragile Queer*.

0. To my straight friends

1. To Ross

2. To Yeva

3. To Daisy

4. To Bridget

5. To all the versions of myself I have been while writing this book

6. To all queers and their struggles, and their joys

X. To you

CONTENTS

Kinsey Scale	11
0. In the Queer Club Are Cops	13
1. 52-Hertz	14
2. /////////////////////////////	15
3. POV: you're gay & useless & it's easier to write a girl a poem than to ask her on a date	16
4. Lazy Daisy	17
5. Boner	18
6. Contactless	19
X. Breakup Poem	20
Kinsey Scale, a Draft	21
0. The Apocalypse	23
1. Death of the Author	24
2. CW Transphobia Hatecrimes Suicide	25
3. Blackbox	26
4. To Be Known	27
5. Notch	28
6. Hither (In The Voice of a Transphobe)	29
X. Over My Dead Body	30
Kinsey Scale for the Emotionally Fragile Queer	32

KINSEY SCALE

0.   Exclusively heterosexual

1.   Predominantly heterosexual, only incidentally homosexual

2.   Predominantly heterosexual, but more than incidentally homosexual

3.   Equally heterosexual and homosexual

4.   Predominantly homosexual, but more than incidentally heterosexual

5.   Predominantly homosexual, only incidentally heterosexual

6.   Exclusively homosexual

X.   No socio-sexual contacts or reactions

0. In the Queer Club Are Cops

Lurking in the corner is a cop. Plain clothes. Pains him to be there but he must. In the crowd is a cop. Dancing out of tune with a hand on batoned hip. Hard to miss. On the stage is a cop. Singing out of contractual obligation. Other cops applaud him. On the sidelines is a cop. Wallflower. Taser-happy. Loosen up. Behind the bar is a cop. Spilling drinks all over his uniform. Hard to pour with one eye on the crowd. In the bathroom is a cop. Acting off his face but refusing to take his face off. He pretends to fix his makeup all night long. Borrows lipstick. Tells all the girlcops how beautiful they are. The drag queen is a cop. She is learning new things about herself. The party never stops. Cops eyeing cops eyeing cops. No queer will ever feel at home again. Not on their watch. They really do believe they're doing a good job. All cops make it home in the morning. All cops.

1. 52-Hertz

Here, in this city, we don't say we're lonely. We just are. Even her, with her endless adventures. Even you, with your friends and insistence. We scrape the barrel for wisdom, but come up empty and out of breath. Count that another bottle drunk, and the same songs are playing over and over and on. But then, come out? For a pint, a drink,

        shots!

She shouts, her face delightfully red and close to yours. Maybe tonight she will hold you, and you will make her cum. A kindness we all know the value of in this economy of gigs and loose plans.

Our generation has the attention span of a five-second news clip. Of towers falling. The splash of an iceberg drowning itself. A dying species. We are motionless, unable to tread water for worry of kicking fish. We were promised mortgages, jobs that don't exist—

Hey! She snaps her fingers. Are you listening? Have you been paying attention? Are you mad? Did I do something wrong? What is happening to us? I thought we were okay, that everything was fine, that we were happy, here

in this city. In every city, and every town, we wail into the aether. Young, but not that young anymore, we remember the millennium. The time before and after. We know joy like orgasms: explosive. Nothing lasts, especially not that happiness of ours. We don't own anything, but we don't mind.

We are endlings,
        each of us
                the last of our kind.

2. ////////////////////////////

I am aaaaaaall line break,
none of that pronoun
weakness. Catch me
if you can, I am a pause.
Untouchable. I am ////////.
Oh, ////? Yeah, I know ////.
Sometimes I'll just be a
single / but more often
than not I am ///////////
///////////////////

/////////////& enough.

3. POV: you're gay & useless & it's easier to write a girl a poem than to ask her on a date

The way you speak, not frequently, but when, with
passionate abandon, and how you listen, largely,
thinking cap on but not to share, not often, no,
it is easier to be kind in silence and make light
of your own darkness when asked. Why then,
why uncomfortable with the spotlight and the
praise, the worry of being judged, but heart on
thumb-through sleeve and poetry like sleight of
hand, what is there to be scared of with a mind

like that, which never stops running, and a laugh
like that, and the courage of a really strong mouse,
or Remy the rat, you know, the one from Ratatouille,
who became a chef despite being a rodent, do you
ever feel small or big like that, where does your wild
heart go when it goes roaming, does it always come
back home, and do you? There are so many things
I'd ask if I thought you might want to answer, oh,
the things I would write if I were a little braver.

4. Lazy Daisy

There's an embroidery stitch called the lazy daisy,
where you wrap a thread around a needle before
sticking it back in to make a wee knot. I often
imagine you lazily wrapping limbs around mine in
my hammock. I feel so sharp these days

I could puncture my bubble and touch you.
Lately every decision has come with a choking
hazard, and I have let my mind roam but
kept my body safe. I would like to be
proud of that one day. I am taking my time

with patience, dragging myself through the eye
of a needle. Dear god, the waiting. I have not
felt free since last February, but I have learned
to stitch a knot with intention, and how to be lazy,

and to let a noose bloom into the soft heart of a daisy.

5. Boner

My garden (where the hamsters are buried) is a season's wet dream. A silly thought: a forearm is just like a flowerbed, it doesn't bend until it snaps. Some things are strong like that, but others sway in the wind & wave.

You think choices are fertile soil for mistakes. Ask the ground for permission to shake it before saying brave things. Worried about which bones you might unearth with your big words. Be still? If we stay here a little longer we'll decay.

We can remain two skeletons, doing what bones do so well. Jumping around in the summer storms and scaring all the neighbours. Spinning circles while you hold me by the radius. Digging up our own graves. I could die like this, already buried

                                            deep below
                                            you.

6. Contactless

No, I'll pay for groceries today,
please. Let me love you. The
world is on the cusp of extinction
and my pasta is to die for. Promise.
We work so well in the kitchen. I keep
my knives sharp and you bring your
cocktail shaker. Get me drunk on you.
So what you don't feel you have a
reason to get up in the morning. This
year has been the closest thing to
starvation, but let me tell you. When
it is over we will feast. Stomp grief
into the ground and toast to dance
floor burials. For now, press your feet
against my inner thighs when they get
cold. I'll scold you, but I won't mean it.
No, don't be silly, put your card away.

X. Breakup Poem

I see a dog wearing booties in the park and all I want to do is tell you about it. There's a fat baby squirrel too, and I think about sending you a photo to convince you I am worth loving. Can I not just swallow up your problems instead and explode? Any fate is better than this one. Yes I know I'm being dramatic – bite me. Please. Take my finger in your mouth and lap me up. Or even if it's just a hug. God, I'm so fucking angry at you it's impossible. Are you not reading through our old messages and changing your mind??? Text me. Yes I know I told you not to message me until I message you, shut up. And anyway, if you showed up at my door I would take you back in a heartbeat. I'm totally gonna get over you soon, though, so hurry. No, scratch that, take your time. It happens, right? The grand gesture. I watch the sun set and want to tell you I am still looking west, that I see you. It doesn't change anything, I know. What a terrible ending to a poem. What a terrible ending.

KINSEY SCALE, A DRAFT

0.   Compulsory heterosexuality

1.   Never Have I Ever kissed a girl hehe

2.   Coming out is a multi-level marketing scam

3.   Greedy bisexuals deserve the world

4.   I want to be you and I want to be with you

5.   They/them hey/when late/then stay/friend stray/bend break/mend

6.   TBD

X.   Queerness is the beginning and the end

0. The Apocalypse

Trans joy is falling from the sky like ash. A dark cloud of the stuff is slowly covering the sun. I watch my shadow fold into itself. There is a siren blaring in the distance. *ALERT. ALERT.* Trans joy has erupted from a supervolcano on a different continent and it is making its way over. Trans joy has already claimed many victims, although we won't know this until later. We will gather in Kai's living room, the big one with the comfy couches and the flags on the ceiling, and refresh Twitter. Wait for news from America. But none will come. Trans joy will have taken them all. Trans joy will block out the light for millennia. We will learn to live in the darkness. There will be other survivors, but we won't reach them for a few years. A quiet world full of trans people living, scarcely, in peace. It is coming. Trans joy is boiling underneath the earth's crust waiting for its opportunity to burst. The violence of the whole affair will startle the planet to its core. Shift us on our axis. Bend. It would make the papers if there were still any in print. *Trans people biggest threat to society in 21st century*, a faded *Guardian* headline will read underneath the layer of soot. Modern prophets. Whistleblowers. They had no idea how right they were. No clue.

1. Death of the Author

telling you   like eating a beautiful meal
digesting it slowly   shitting it out
and excitedly presenting it on a silver platter

'here! you can have it'

telling you   and then again   and again
and over   telling you   in slow motion
a balloon   swelling   then *pop!*

telling you   and then slowly dissolving
into the floor   becoming less than invisible
untouchable   and so lonely

telling you   tearing something beautiful
out of myself   and seeing it there
mangled   regretting it

letting you   kill me
allowing you the privilege   of my death

tell me   I have no right to live

2. CW Transphobia Hatecrimes Suicide

the ease with which   we discuss
the death of us   the bodies dis
membered   the blood spilled
in cursive   it is hardly violent
anymore   just another day
at the office   just another
body   just another
statement   it is all we are
bodies and   statements
bodies and   statements
bodies

once loved   so gently
held queerly   sung about in
private messages   touched
in group effort   to stave off
early death   we are bodies
that do not hold   much
no pockets   just holes
that maybe once   were holy
I am no saint   my fingers cure
so little but   pleasure so much

I know my love   is not enough
I know I cannot   catch   the body
when it falls   nor stop it
from jumping   I know my poetry
is not a reason   but let me write us
not an obituary   but a legacy
      where we get caught

3. Blackbox

come here with your rage

I know you keep it close to your chest   for safekeeping
I do the same   but   it cannot live there forever
it is too precious to hide away like that   let it breathe
let it set fire to the world   the flames
will lap up the earth thirstily   ruin everything
you were promised   faster than redemption ever could

when your fingers have turned   to charred blisters
scorched fingerprints   skin too fragile to put ink to page
open up your rage   take apart the darkened exoskeleton
do not discard   cherish it   you were someone before
you were burdened   but you cannot go back

examine it   watch the tears   come from nowhere
then harden into bone   this is the make of you
a beautiful thing   inside a tragedy   inside a war

and yet you are whole   burning   but whole

I will not tell you   to douse yourself   though
if you are going to burn   take the world down with you
we cannot redeem it   but we can rebuild

4. To Be Known

sometimes violence   is gentle
rocked you to sleep   when you were little
sometimes our tragedies   are so soft
you do not have to die   to be buried
or be abandoned   to be forgotten
        but you do have to be known

each story that begins   bright-coloured
ends with trauma   to be queer is to be a narrative
to be a headline   is to be someone
martyrs get legacies   but queer kids get
a hundred corpses   we shed ourselves of
        on our way to our heavens

here is one reality   I am happy now
that is a legacy too   I count my blessings
& remember a death wish   isn't born from a safe mind
you are so young   & have seen so many endings
life is cutting you short   from both sides
        you don't have to listen to both sides

sometimes violence is   a balanced debate
an open mind   an echoless chamber
I love the sound   of my own voice
and yours   speaking truth
we have nothing   to say for ourselves
        we have nothing to prove

5. Notch

if you still love   the warmth of her embrace
despite everything   crawl back through the years
on your dark days   into your mother's loveliness
ignore how she holds you   like a daughter
strokes your hair   wishing it was longer

remember this   being fallible doesn't mean you are at fault
there may come a time when you blow away your straw home
there may not   we all walk as tall as we are   & grow
sometimes violence is   measuring yourself against the wall
of your childhood home   sometimes it is a reclamation

to write yourself   for the first time   on an old place

6. Hither (In The Voice of a Transphobe)

doesn't it seem a bit callous to walk there   at this moment
to choose this point in time to exist   have you considered
living on the edge of something less tall   less beckoning

how about closing the distance   getting off that high horse
how about it?   come to me with open arms
I will greet you   by ripping the arson from your heart

cut short your explosive potential   make you swallow your rage
if you wish to dine at this table   you better sit up straight
watch that mouth of yours   love the name we gave

we like our traditions kept safe   this will be the price you pay
you poor thing   you will never have to feel that dark anger again
don't you want to believe   the world is softer

the option of bliss lies within the capture   of your bony knuckles
fists to fists   allow me   to come knocking
open on up babe   relax your shoulder

                                                                              relax

X. OVER MY DEAD BODY

bury me in an echo chamber
listen hear a thousand voices
in agreement over who I was
and always have been

burn me warmly
my ashes gendered with love
not malice no postmortem
on my intentions when I die

bury me how I lived
among those I stood with
not those who murdered me
eulogise them instead

burn me into the folklore
of my people a poet
too in love to let the intolerance
of others harm their sacred friends

when it is time do me this last favour
sink me in waters that never rippled
with the resonance of hatred
dig up turf not colonised by language

in this place (we'll call it paradise)

raise from fertile flesh a community of sinners who have never heard of sin grow them a whole body of poetry that doesn't speak of pain let my name be forgotten when it is time to leave behind the memory of war poets and bury me
                                             in peace

KINSEY SCALE FOR THE EMOTIONALLY FRAGILE QUEER

0. It was knowing emptiness that made me a glutton.

1. 'Finding girls pretty is totally normal.'

2. I met a girl and one day, I noticed a strand of hair falling out of her messy bun, brushing down the nape of her neck onto her shoulders. I didn't know what it was but I knew it wasn't normal.

3. Queerness has no beginning and no end.

4. Predominantly homosexual, but more than incidentally heterosexual. Predominantly homosexual, but more than heterosexual. Predominantly homosexual, more than heterosexual. Homosexual, more than heterosexual. Homosexual, more than. homosexual, more.

               Homosexual.

5. Some queer boys never get to feel the touch of another boy in their life. Queerness does not inherently liberate us. We do what we can.

6. Most queer adults did not get to be queer children. We did not get to queerly come of age, did not get queer teenage years. We relive these days through impossible nostalgia for a time that never was. For the last day of class when summer starts and you have your first crush and she kisses you in late August under a baby boy blue sky and you whisper that you are not a girl nor a boy and she helps you cut your hair and after, no one beats you up on your way home. When you get there, you tell your parents you are gay or queer or trans and they say, *we love you, we love you, we love you.*

X. Queerness is not measured in tally marks on a wall, there is no one keeping score. Welcome home.

We love you,

we love you,

we love you.

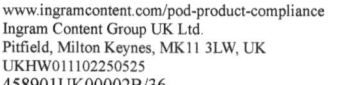

www.ingramcontent.com/pod-product-compliance
Ingram Content Group UK Ltd.
Pitfield, Milton Keynes, MK11 3LW, UK
UKHW011102250525
458901UK00002B/36